Best Vegan Cookbook 2021

Best Vegan Main-Course Recipes for Beginners

Sommario

Introduction

Becoming a vegetarian can be a lifestyle that brings several advantages both for the protection of animals and for your health, in fact a vegetarian diet can help you stay healthy and avoid chronic diseases such as diabetes. you choose to abolish all forms of meat including pork, chicken, shells, fish, game and beef.

some still prefer to consume animal by-products and others who, on the other hand, are more extremist, also eliminate these from their diet. if this world intrigues you, I invite you to search for your favorite dish by consulting our fantastic book, Bon Appetit.

Main course

Baked Spinach and Butternut Squash

Ingredients

1 ½ pounds butternut squash, peeled and cut into 1-inch chunks

½ red onion, thinly sliced

¼ cup water

½ vegetable stock cube, crumbled 1 tbsp. extra virgin olive oil

½ tsp cumin

½ tsp annatto seeds

½ tsp cayenne pepper

½ tsp hot chili powderBlack pepper

½ pound fresh spinach, roughly chopped

Put all of the ingredients in a slow cooker except the last one. Top with handfuls of spinach and stuff the slow cooker with it.

If you can't fit it all in at once, let the first batch cook first and add some more spinach.

Cook for 3or 4 hours on medium until squash become soft. Scrape the sides and serve.

Roasted Kale and Rutabaga

Ingredients

1 ½ pounds rutabaga ,peeled and cut into 1-inch chunks

½ onion, thinly sliced

¼ cup water

½ vegetable stock cube, crumbled 1 tbsp. extra virgin olive oil

½ tsp cumin

½ tsp jalapeno peppers, minced

½ tsp paprika

½ tsp hot chili powderBlack pepper

½ pound fresh kale, roughly chopped

Put all of the ingredients in a slow cooker except the last one.Top with handfuls of kale and stuff the slow cooker with it.

If you can't fit it all in at once, let the first batch cook first and add some more kale.

Cook for 3 or 4 hours on medium until rutabaga become soft. Scrape the sides and serve.

Baked Watercress and Summer Squash

Ingredients

1 ½ pounds summer squash, peeled and cut into 1-inch chunks

½ red onion, thinly sliced

¼ cup water

½ vegetable stock cube, crumbled 1 tbsp. sesame oil

½ tsp Chinese 5 spice powder

½ tsp Sichuan Peppercorns

½ tsp hot chili powder Black pepper

½ pound fresh watercress, roughly chopped

Put all of the ingredients in a slow cooker except the last one. Top with handfuls of watercress and stuff the slow cooker with it. If you can't fit it all in at once, let the first batch cook first and add some more watercress.

Cook for 3 or 4 hours on medium until summer squash become

soft. Scrape the sides and serve.

Spicy and Tangy Roasted Spinach & Purple Yam

Ingredients

1 ½ pounds purple yam, peeled and cut into 1-inch chunks

½ onion, thinly sliced

¼ cup water

½ vegetable stock cube, crumbled 1 tbsp. extra virgin olive oil

½ tsp cumin

½ tsp annatto seeds

½ tsp cayenne pepper

½ tsp lime juice Black pepper

½ pound fresh spinach, roughly chopped

Put all of the ingredients in a slow cooker except the last one. Top with handfuls of spinach and stuff the slow cooker with it.

If you can't fit it all in at once, let the first batch cook first and add some more spinach.

Cook for 3 or 4 hours on medium until the root vegetables become soft.

Scrape the sides and serve.

Curried Kale and Rutabaga

Ingredients

1 ½ pounds Rutabaga, peeled and cut into 1-inch chunks

½ onion, thinly sliced

¼ cup water

½ vegetable stock cube, crumbled 1 tbsp. extra virgin olive oil

½ tsp cumin

½ tsp ground coriander

½ tsp garam masala

½ tsp hot chili powderBlack pepper

½ pound fresh kale, roughly chopped

Put all of the ingredients in a slow cooker except the last one.Top with handfuls of kale and stuff the slow cooker with it.

If you can't fit it all in at once, let the first batch cook first and add some more kale.

Cook for 3 or 4 hours on medium until root vegetables become soft. Scrape the sides and serve.

Spicy Roasted Spinach and Carrots

Ingredients

1 ½ pounds carrots, peeled and cut into 1-inch chunks

½ onion, thinly sliced

¼ cup water

½ vegetable stock cube, crumbled 1 tbsp. extra virgin olive oil

½ tsp cumin

½ tsp annatto seeds

½ tsp cayenne pepper

½ tsp lime
juice   Black
pepper

½ pound fresh spinach, roughly chopped

Put all of the ingredients in a slow cooker except the last one. Top with handfuls of spinach and stuff the slow cooker with it.

If you can't fit it all in at once, let the first batch cook first and add some more spinach.

Cook for 3 or 4 hours on medium until root vegetables become soft. Scrape the sides and serve.

Buttered Potatoes and Spinach

Ingredients

1 ½ pounds red potatoes, peeled and cut into 1-inch chunks

½ onion, thinly sliced

¼ cup water

½ vegetable stock cube, crumbled2 tbsp. salted butter

½ tsp herbs de Provence

½ tsp thyme

½ tsp hot chili powderBlack pepper

½ pound fresh spinach, roughly chopped

Put all of the ingredients in a slow cooker except the last one.Top with handfuls of spinach and stuff the slow cooker with it.

If you can't fit it all in at once, let the first batch cook first and addsome more spinach.

Cook for 3or 4 hours on medium until potatoes become soft. Scrape the sides and serve.

Roasted Turnips and Collard Greens

Ingredients

1 ½ pounds turnips, peeled and cut into 1-inch chunks

½ onion, thinly sliced

¼ cup water

½ vegetable stock cube, crumbled 1 tbsp. extra virgin olive oil

2 tsp. garlic, minced

½ tsp lime juice

½ tsp hot chili powderBlack pepper

½ pound fresh Collard greens, roughly chopped

Put all of the ingredients in a slow cooker except the last one.

Top with handfuls of collard greens and stuff the slow cooker with it. If you can't fit it all in at once, let the first batch cook first and add some more collard greens.

Cook for 3or 4 hours on medium until turnips become soft. Scrape the sides and serve.

Roasted Vegan-Buttered Mustard Greens Carrots

Ingredients

1 ½ pounds carrots, peeled and cut into 1-inch chunks

½ onion, thinly sliced

¼ cup water

½ vegetable stock cube, crumbled 1 tbsp. butter

1 tsp garlic, minced

½ tsp lemon
juice   Black
pepper

½ pound fresh mustard greens, roughly chopped

Put all of the ingredients in a slow cooker except the last one.

Top with handfuls of mustard greens and stuff the slow cooker with it. If you can't fit it all in at once, let the first batch cook first and add some more mustard greens.

Cook for 3 or 4 hours on medium until carrots become soft.

Scrape the sides and serve.

Baked Broccoli and Swiss Chard

Ingredients

1 ½ pounds broccoli florets

½ onion, thinly sliced

¼ cup water

½ vegetable stock cube, crumbled 1 tbsp. extra virgin olive oil

½ tsp cumin

½ tsp hot chili powderBlack pepper

½ pound fresh Swiss chard, roughly chopped

Put all of the ingredients in a slow cooker except the last one. Top with handfuls of Swiss chard and stuff the slow cooker with it.If you can't fit it all in at once, let the first batch cook first and add some more Swiss chard.

Cook for 3or 4 hours on medium until broccoli become soft. Scrape the sides and serve.

Smoky Roasted Swiss Chard and Cauliflower

Ingredients

1 ½ pounds cauliflower, peeled and cut into 1-inch chunks

½ red onion, thinly sliced

¼ cup water

½ vegetable stock cube, crumbled 1 tbsp. extra virgin olive oil

½ tsp cumin

½ tsp hot chili powderBlack pepper

½ pound fresh Swiss chard, roughly chopped

Put all of the ingredients in a slow cooker except the last one. Top with handfuls of Swiss chard and stuff the slow cooker with it. If you can't fit it all in at once, let the first batch cook first and add some more Swiss chard.

Cook for 3or 4 hours on medium until potatoes become soft. Scrape the sides and serve.

Roasted Italian Beets and Kale

Ingredients

1 ½ pounds beets, peeled and cut into 1-inch chunks

½ red onion, thinly sliced

¼ cup water

½ vegetable stock cube, crumbled 1 tbsp. extra virgin

olive oil

½ tsp Italian seasoning Black pepper

½ pound fresh kale, roughly chopped

Put all of the ingredients in a slow cooker except the last one. Top with handfuls of kale and stuff the slow cooker with it.

If you can't fit it all in at once, let the first batch cook first and add some more kale.

Cook for 3 or 4 hours on medium until beets become soft. Scrape the sides and serve.

Roasted Microgreens and Potatoes

Ingredients

1 ½ pounds potatoes, peeled and cut into 1-inch chunks

½ onion, thinly sliced

¼ cup water

½ vegetable stock cube, crumbled1 tbsp. olive oil

½ tsp minced
ginger 2 sprigs
lemon grass

½ tsp green onions, minced

½ tsp hot chili
powderBlack pepper

½ pound Microgreens, roughly chopped

Put all of the ingredients in a slow cooker except the last one.

Top with handfuls of Microgreens and stuff the slow cooker

with it. If you can't fit it all in at once, let the first batch cook first and add some more Microgreens.

Cook for 3or 4 hours on medium until potatoes become soft. Scrape the sides and serve.

Roasted Microgreens with Olives

Ingredients

1 ½ pounds potatoes, peeled and cut into 1-inch chunks

½ green olives, thinly sliced

¼ cup water

½ vegetable stock cube, crumbled 1 tbsp. extra virgin olive oil

½ tsp cumin

½ tsp hot chili powderBlack pepper

½ pound fresh microgreens, roughly chopped

Put all of the ingredients in a slow cooker except the last one.

Top with handfuls of microgreens and stuff the slow cooker with it. If you can't fit it all in at once, let the first batch cook first and add some more microgreens.

Cook for 3or 4 hours on medium until potatoes become soft.

Scrape the sides and serve.

Roasted Spinach & Broccoli with Jalapeno

Ingredients

1 ½ pounds broccoli florets

½ onion, thinly sliced

¼ cup water

½ vegetable stock cube, crumbled 1 tbsp. extra virgin olive oil

½ tsp cumin

8 jalapeno peppers, finely chopped 1 ancho chili

½ tsp hot chili powder Black pepper

½ pound fresh spinach, roughly chopped

Put all of the ingredients in a slow cooker except the last one. Top with handfuls of spinach and stuff the slow cooker with it.

If you can't fit it all in at once, let the first batch cook first and add some more spinach.

Cook for 3 or 4 hours on medium until broccoli become soft. Scrape the sides and serve.

Roasted Curried Endives and Potatoes

Ingredients

1 ½ pounds potatoes, peeled and cut into 1-inch chunks

½ onion, thinly sliced

¼ cup water

½ vegetable stock cube, crumbled 1 tbsp. extra virgin olive oil

½ tsp cumin

½ tsp ground coriander

½ tsp garam masala

½ tsp hot chili powderBlack pepper

½ pound fresh endives, roughly chopped

Put all of the ingredients in a slow cooker except the last one.Top with handfuls of endives and stuff the slow cooker with it.

If you can't fit it all in at once, let the first batch cook first and add some more endives.

Cook for 3 or 4 hours on medium until potatoes become soft. Scrape the sides and serve.

Spicy Baked Swiss Chard and Cauliflower

Ingredients

1 ½ pounds cauliflower florets, blanched (dipped in boiling waterthen dipped in ice water)

½ cup bean sprouts, rinsed

½ cup water

½ vegetable stock cube, crumbled1 tbsp. sesame oil

½ tsp Thai chili paste

½ tsp Sriracha hot sauce

½ tsp hot chili powder

2 Thai bird chilies, mincedBlack pepper

½ pound fresh Swiss chard, roughly chopped

Put all of the ingredients in a slow cooker except the last one. Top with handfuls of Swiss chard and stuff the slow cooker with it.If you can't fit it all in at once, let the first batch cook first and add some more Swiss chard.

Cook for 3 or 4 hours on medium until potatoes become soft. Scrape the sides and serve.

Spicy Watercress and Turnips

Ingredients

1 ½ pounds turnips, peeled and cut into 1-inch chunks

½ onion, thinly sliced

¼ cup water

½ vegetable stock cube, crumbled1 tbsp. sesame oil

½ tsp chili garlic paste

½ tsp Sichuan peppercorns 1 star anise

2 Thai bird chilies, minced Black pepper

½ pound fresh Watercress, roughly chopped

Put all of the ingredients in a slow cooker except the last one. Top with handfuls of spinach and stuff the slow cooker with it.

If you can't fit it all in at once, let the first batch cook first and add some more watercress.

Cook for 3 or 4 hours on medium until watercress become soft. Scrape the sides and serve.

Thai Carrots and Collard Greens

Ingredients

1 ½ pounds carrots, peeled and cut into 1-inch chunks

½ onion, thinly sliced

¼ cup water

½ vegetable stock cube, crumbled 1 tbsp. extra virgin olive oil

1 tbsp. sesame oil

½ tsp Thai chili paste

½ tsp Sriracha hot sauce

½ tsp hot chili powder

2 Thai bird chilies, minced Black pepper

½ pound collard greens, roughly chopped

Put all of the ingredients in a slow cooker except the last one.

Top with handfuls of collard greens and stuff the slow cooker with it. If you can't fit it all in at once, let the first batch cook first and add some more collard greens.

Cook for 3or 4 hours on medium until carrots become soft. Scrape the sides and serve.

Roasted Swiss Chard and Sweet Potatoes

Ingredients

½ pound purple yam, peeled and cut into 1-inch chunks

1 pound sweet potatoes, peeled and cut into 1-inch chunks

½ onion, thinly sliced

¼ cup water

½ vegetable stock cube, crumbled 1 tbsp. extra virgin olive oil

Black pepper

½ pound fresh Swiss chard, roughly chopped

Put all of the ingredients in a slow cooker except the last one. Top with handfuls of Swiss chard and stuff the slow cooker with it. If you can't fit it all in at once, let the first batch cook first and add some more Swiss chard.

Cook for 3or 4 hours on medium until potatoes become soft. Scrape the sides and serve.

Baked White Yam and Spinach

Ingredients

½ pounds potatoes, peeled and cut into 1-inch chunks

½ pounds white yam, peeled and cut into 1-inch chunks

½ pounds carrots, peeled and cut into 1-inch chunks

½ red onion, thinly sliced

¼ cup water

½ vegetable stock cube, crumbled 1 tbsp. extra virgin olive oil

½ tsp cumin

½ tsp ground coriander

½ tsp garam masala

½ tsp cayenne pepperBlack pepper

½ pound fresh spinach, roughly chopped

Put all of the ingredients in a slow cooker except the last one. Top with handfuls of spinach and stuff the slow cooker with it.

If you can't fit it all in at once, let the first batch cook first and add some more spinach.

Cook for 3 or 4 hours on medium until potatoes become soft. Scrape the sides and serve.

Hungarian Microgreens and Turnips

Ingredients

½ pound turnips, peeled and cut into 1-inch chunks

½ pound carrots, peeled and cut into 1-inch chunks

½ pound parsnips, peeled and cut into 1-inch chunks

½ red onion, thinly sliced

¼ cup water

½ vegetable stock cube, crumbled 1 tbsp. extra virgin olive oil

½ tsp paprika powder

½ tsp. chili powder Black pepper

½ pound fresh microgreens, roughly chopped

Put all of the ingredients in a slow cooker except the last one.

Top with handfuls of microgreens and stuff the slow cooker

with it. If you can't fit it all in at once, let the first batch cook first and add some more microgreens.

Cook for 3or 4 hours on medium until turnips become soft. Scrape the sides and serve.

Simple Baked Spinach & Broccoli

Ingredients

1 ½ pounds broccoli ,peeled and cut into 1-inch chunks

½ red onion, thinly sliced

¼ cup vegetable stock

1 tbsp. extra virgin olive oil

½ tsp Italian seasoning

½ tsp hot chili powderBlack pepper

½ pound fresh spinach, roughly chopped

Put all of the ingredients in a slow cooker except the last one.Top with handfuls of spinach and stuff the slow cooker with it.

If you can't fit it all in at once, let the first batch cook first and addsome more spinach.

Cook for 3or 4 hours on medium until broccoli become soft. Scrape the sides and serve.

Southeast Asian Baked Turnip Greens & Carrots

Ingredients

½ pound turnips, peeled and cut into 1-inch chunks

½ pound carrots, peeled and cut into 1-inch chunks

½ pound parsnips, peeled and cut into 1-inch chunks

½ red onion, thinly sliced

½ cup vegetable broth

1 tbsp. extra virgin olive oil

½ tsp minced ginger 2 stalks lemon grass

8 cloves garlic, mincedBlack pepper

½ pound fresh turnip greens, roughly chopped

Put all of the ingredients in a slow cooker except the last one.

Top with handfuls of turnip greens and stuff the slow cooker with it. If you can't fit it all in at once, let the first batch cook first and add some more turnip greens.

Cook for 3or 4 hours on medium until turnips become soft. Scrape the sides and serve.

Roasted Endives and Brussels Sprouts

Ingredients

1 ½ pounds brussel sprouts, peeled and cut into 1-inch chunks

½ red onion, thinly sliced

¼ cup water

½ vegetable stock cube, crumbled 1 tbsp. extra virgin olive oil

½ tsp hot chili powderBlack pepper

½ pound endives, roughly chopped

Put all of the ingredients in a slow cooker except the last one.Top with handfuls of endives and stuff the slow cooker with it.

If you can't fit it all in at once, let the first batch cook first and addsome more endives.

Cook for 3 hours on medium until brussel sprouts become soft.Scrape the sides and serve.

Curried Watercress and Potatoes

Ingredients

1 ½ pounds potatoes, peeled and cut into 1-inch chunks

½ onion, thinly sliced

¼ cup water

½ vegetable stock cube, crumbled 1 tbsp. extra virgin olive oil

½ tsp cumin

½ tsp ground coriander

½ tsp garam masala

½ tsp hot chili powderBlack pepper

½ pound fresh Watercress, roughly chopped

Put all of the ingredients in a slow cooker except the last one. Top with handfuls of watercress and stuff the slow cooker with it. If you can't fit it all in at once, let the first batch cook first and add some more watercress.

Cook for 3 or 4 hours on medium until potatoes become soft. Scrape the sides and serve.

Curried Sweet Potatoes and Swiss Chard

Ingredients

1 ½ pounds sweet potatoes, peeled and cut into 1-inch chunks

½ onion, thinly sliced

¼ cup water

½ vegetable stock cube, crumbled 1 tbsp. extra virgin olive oil

½ tsp cumin

½ tsp ground coriander

½ tsp garam masala

½ tsp hot chili powderBlack pepper

½ pound swiss chard, roughly chopped

Put all of the ingredients in a slow cooker except the last one. Top with handfuls of swiss chard and stuff the slow cooker with it.If you can't fit it all in at once, let the first batch cook first and add some more swiss chard.

Cook for 3 or 4 hours on medium until sweet potatoes become soft. Scrape the sides and serve.

Jalapeno Kale and Parsnips

Ingredients

1 ½ pounds parsnips, peeled and cut into 1-inch chunks

½ red onion, thinly sliced

¼ cup water

½ vegetable stock cube, crumbled 1 tbsp. extra virgin olive oil

½ tsp cumin

½ tsp jalapeno pepper, minced 1 ancho chili, minced

Black pepper

½ pound Kale, roughly chopped

Put all of the ingredients in a slow cooker except the last one. Top with handfuls of kale and stuff the slow cooker with it.

If you can't fit it all in at once, let the first batch cook first and add some more Kale.

Cook for 3 or 4 hours on medium until parsnips become soft. Scrape the sides and serve.

Collard Greens and Broccoli in Chili Garlic Sauce

Ingredients

1 ½ pounds carrots, peeled and cut into 1-inch chunks

½ pound broccoli, peeled and cut into 1-inch chunks

½ onion, thinly sliced

¼ cup water

½ vegetable stock cube, crumbled1 tbsp. sesame oil

½ tsp chili garlic sauce

½ tsp. lime juice

½ tsp. minced green onionsBlack pepper

½ pound collard greens, roughly chopped

Put all of the ingredients in a slow cooker except the last one.

Top with handfuls of collard greens and stuff the slow cooker with it. If you can't fit it all in at once, let the first batch cook first and add some more collard greens.

Cook for 3or 4 hours on medium until carrots become soft. Scrape the sides and serve.

Spicy Choy Sum and Broccoli

Ingredients

1 pound broccoli, peeled and cut into 1-inch chunks

½ pound button mushrooms, sliced

½ onion, thinly sliced

¼ cup water

½ vegetable stock cube, crumbled 1 tbsp. sesame oil

½ tsp Chinese five spice powder

½ tsp Sichuan peppercorns

½ tsp hot chili powder Black pepper

½ pound choy sum, roughly chopped

Put all of the ingredients in a slow cooker except the last one. Top with handfuls of choy sum and stuff the slow cooker with it. If you can't fit it all in at once, let the first batch cook first and add some more choy sum.

Cook for 3or 4 hours on medium until broccoli become soft. Scrape the sides and serve.

Mustard Greens and Shitake Mushroom

Ingredients

1 ½ pounds cauliflower, peeled and cut into 1-inch chunks

½ pound shitake mushrooms, sliced

½ red onion, thinly sliced

¼ cup vegetable stock
2 tbsp. sesame seed
oil

½ tsp vinegar

½ tsp garlic,
minced Black
pepper

½ pound fresh mustard greens, roughly chopped

Put all of the ingredients in a slow cooker except the last one.

Top with handfuls of mustard greens and stuff the slow cooker with it. If you can't fit it all in at once, let the first batch cook first and add some more mustard greens.

Cook for 3 or 4 hours on medium until cauliflower become soft. Scrape the sides and serve.

Kale and Potatoes in Pesto Sauce

Ingredients

1 ½ pounds potatoes, peeled and cut into 1-inch chunks

½ onion, thinly sliced

¼ cup vegetable stock

1 tbsp. extra virgin olive
oil2 tbsp. pesto sauce

Black pepper

½ pound fresh Kale, roughly chopped

Put all of the ingredients in a slow cooker except the last one. Top with handfuls of Kale and stuff the slow cooker with it.

If you can't fit it all in at once, let the first batch cook first and add some more Kale.

Cook for 3 or 4 hours on medium until potatoes become soft. Scrape the sides and serve.

Curried Rutabaga and Collard Greens

Ingredients

1 ½ pounds rutabaga , peeled and cut into 1-inch chunks

½ onion, thinly sliced

¼ cup vegetable stock

1 tbsp. extra virgin olive
oil 2 tbsp. red curry
powder Black pepper

½ pound fresh collard greens, roughly chopped

Put all of the ingredients in a slow cooker except the last one.

Top with handfuls of collard greens and stuff the slow cooker with it. If you can't fit it all in at once, let the first batch cook first and add some more collard greens.

Cook for 3 or 4 hours on medium until rutabaga become soft. Scrape the sides and serve.

Turnip Greens and Kohlrabi in Pesto Sauce

Ingredients

1 ½ pounds kohlrabi,peeled and cut into 1-inch chunks

½ onion, thinly sliced

¼ cup vegetable stock

1 tbsp. extra virgin olive
oil2 tbsp. pesto sauce

Black pepper

½ pound fresh Turnip Greens, roughly chopped

Put all of the ingredients in a slow cooker except the last one.

Top with handfuls of Turnip Greens and stuff the slow cooker with it.If you can't fit it all in at once, let the first batch cook first and add some more Turnip Greens.

Cook for 3or 4 hours on medium until kohlrabi become soft. Scrape the sides and serve.

Swiss Chard and Yam in Pesto Sauce

Ingredients

1 ½ pounds yam, peeled and cut into 1-inch chunks

½ red onion, thinly sliced

¼ cup vegetable stock

2 tbsp. extra virgin olive
oil3 tbsp. pesto sauce

Black pepper

½ pound fresh Swiss Chard, roughly chopped

Put all of the ingredients in a slow cooker except the last one.

Top with handfuls of Swiss Chard and stuff the slow cooker with it. If you can't fit it all in at once, let the first batch cook first and add some more Swiss Chard.

Cook for 3 or 4 hours on medium until yam become soft. Scrape the sides and serve.

Bok Choy and Kohlrabi in Chili Garlic Sauce

Ingredients

1 ½ pounds kohlrabi, peeled and cut into 1-inch chunks

½ onion, thinly sliced

¼ cup vegetable stock 1 tbsp. sesame oil

4 cloves garlic, minced

2 tbsp. chili garlic sauce Black pepper

½ pound fresh Bok Choy, roughly chopped

Put all of the ingredients in a slow cooker except the last one. Top with handfuls of Bok Choy and stuff the slow cooker with it. If you can't fit it all in at once, let the first batch cook first and add some more Bok Choy.

Cook for 3 or 4 hours on medium until kohlrabi become soft. Scrape the sides and serve.

Slow Cooked Turnip Greens and Butternut Squash

Ingredients

1 ½ pounds butternut squash, peeled and cut into 1-inch chunks

½ onion, thinly sliced

¼ cup vegetable stock

1 tbsp. extra virgin olive
oilBlack pepper

½ pound fresh Turnip greens, roughly chopped

Put all of the ingredients in a slow cooker except the last one.Top with handfuls of spinach and stuff the slow cooker with it.

If you can't fit it all in at once, let the first batch cook first and addsome more spinach.

Cook for 3or 4 hours on medium until butternut squash become soft.Scrape the sides and serve.

Slow Cooked Kale and Summer Squash

Ingredients

1 ½ pounds summer squash, peeled and cut into 1-inch chunks

½ onion, thinly sliced

¼ cup vegetable stock

1 tbsp. extra virgin olive oil2 tbsp. pesto sauce

Black pepper

½ pound fresh Kale, roughly chopped

Put all of the ingredients in a slow cooker except the last one.Top with handfuls of kale and stuff the slow cooker with it.

If you can't fit it all in at once, let the first batch cook first and addsome more kale.

Cook for 3or 4 hours on medium until summer squash become soft.Scrape the sides and serve.

Slow Cooked Endives and Winter Squash in Pesto Sauce

Ingredients

1 ½ pounds winter squash, peeled and cut into 1-inch chunks

½ onion, thinly sliced

¼ cup vegetable stock

1 tbsp. extra virgin olive
oil2 tbsp. pesto sauce

Black pepper

½ pound fresh Endive, roughly chopped

Put all of the ingredients in a slow cooker except the last one. Top with handfuls of endive and stuff the slow cooker with it.

If you can't fit it all in at once, let the first batch cook first and addsome more endive.

Cook for 3or 4 hours on medium until winter squash become soft. Scrape the sides and serve.

Slow-cooked Endives and Brussel Sprouts

Ingredients

1 ½ pounds brussel sprouts

½ onion, thinly sliced

¼ cup vegetable stock

1 tbsp. extra virgin olive
oilBlack pepper

½ pound fresh endives, roughly chopped

Put all of the ingredients in a slow cooker except the last one.Top with handfuls of endives and stuff the slow cooker with it.

If you can't fit it all in at once, let the first batch cook first and addsome more endives.

Cook for 3 hours on medium until brussel sprouts become soft.Scrape the sides and serve.

Slow-cooked Microgreens and Potatoes

Ingredients

1 ½ pounds potatoes, peeled and cut into 1-inch chunks

½ onion, thinly sliced

¼ cup vegetable stock

1 tbsp. extra virgin olive
oil 1 tsp. Italian
seasoning Black pepper

½ pound microgreens, roughly chopped

Put all of the ingredients in a slow cooker except the last one.

Top with handfuls of microgreens and stuff the slow cooker with it. If you can't fit it all in at once, let the first batch cook first and add some more microgreens.

Cook for 3or 4 hours on medium until potatoes become soft. Scrape the sides and serve.

Buttery Swiss Chard and Turnips

Ingredients

1 ½ pounds turnips, peeled and cut into 1-inch chunks

½ onion, thinly sliced

¼ cup vegetable stock

4 tbsp. vegan butter or margarine 2 tbsp. lime juice

3 cloves garlic, minced Black pepper

½ pound fresh swiss chard, roughly chopped

Put all of the ingredients in a slow cooker except the last one. Top with handfuls of swiss chard and stuff the slow cooker with it. If you can't fit it all in at once, let the first batch cook first and add some more swiss chard.

Cook for 3 or 4 hours on medium until turnips become soft. Scrape the sides and serve.

Buttery Watercress and Parsnips

Ingredients

1 ½ pounds parsnips, peeled and cut into 1-inch chunks

½ onion, thinly sliced

¼ cup vegetable stock

4 tbsp. melted vegan
butter2 tbsp. lemon juice

Black pepper

½ pound fresh Watercress, roughly chopped

Put all of the ingredients in a slow cooker except the last one. Top with handfuls of watercress and stuff the slow cooker with it. If you can't fit it all in at once, let the first batch cook first and addsome more Watercress.

Cook for 3or 4 hours on medium until parsnips become soft. Scrape the sides and serve.

Slow Cooked Chinese Style Choy Sum & Carrots

Ingredients

1 ½ pounds carrots, peeled and cut into 1-inch chunks

½ onion, thinly sliced

¼ cup vegetable stock1 tbsp. sesame oil

2 tbsp. hoi sin sauceBlack pepper

½ pound choy sum, roughly chopped

Put all of the ingredients in a slow cooker except the last one. Top with handfuls of choy sum and stuff the slow cooker with it. If you can't fit it all in at once, let the first batch cook first and addsome more choy sum.

Cook for 3or 4 hours on medium until carrots become soft. Scrape the sides and serve.

Slow Cooked Bok Choy and Carrots

Ingredients

1 ½ pounds carrots, peeled and cut into 1-inch chunks

½ onion, thinly sliced

¼ cup vegetable stock 1 tbsp. sesame oil

1 tbsp. canola oil

2 tbsp. hoi sin sauce Black pepper

½ pound fresh Bok Choy, roughly chopped

Put all of the ingredients in a slow cooker except the last one. Top with handfuls of bok choy and stuff the slow cooker with it.

If you can't fit it all in at once, let the first batch cook first and add some more bok choy.

Cook for 3or 4 hours on medium until carrots become soft. Scrape the sides and serve.

Slow Cooked Micro greens and Potatoes

Ingredients

1 ½ pounds potatoes, peeled and cut into 1-inch chunks

½ onion, thinly sliced

¼ cup vegetable stock

2 tbsp. extra virgin olive
oil1 tsp. annatto seeds

1 tsp. cumin

1 tsp. lime
juice Black
pepper

½ pound fresh Micro greens, roughly chopped

Put all of the ingredients in a slow cooker except the last one.

Top with handfuls of micro greens and stuff the slow cooker with it. If you can't fit it all in at once, let the first batch cook first and add some more micro greens.

Cook for 3or 4 hours on medium until potatoes become soft.

Scrape the sides and serve.

Slow Cooked Mustard Greens and Sweet Potatoes

Ingredients

1 ½ pounds sweet potatoes, peeled and cut into 1-inch chunks

½ onion, thinly sliced

¼ cup vegetable stock

1 tbsp. extra virgin olive
oil2 tbsp. pesto sauce

Black pepper

½ pound fresh mustard greens, roughly chopped

Put all of the ingredients in a slow cooker except the last one.

Top with handfuls of mustard greens and stuff the slow cooker with it. If you can't fit it all in at once, let the first batch cook first and add some more mustard greens.

Cook for 3or 4 hours on medium until sweet potatoes become soft. Scrape the sides and serve.

Slow Cooked Red Cabbage and Potatoes

Ingredients

1 ½ pounds potatoes, peeled and cut into 1-inch chunks

½ onion, thinly sliced

¼ cup vegetable stock

1 tbsp. extra virgin olive
oilBlack pepper

½ pound fresh Red cabbage, roughly chopped

Put all of the ingredients in a slow cooker except the last one.

Top with handfuls of red cabbage and stuff the slow cooker with it. If you can't fit it all in at once, let the first batch cook first and add some more red cabbage.

Cook for 3or 4 hours on medium until potatoes become soft. Scrape the sides and serve.

Slow Cooked Cabbage and Rutabaga

Ingredients

1 ½ pounds rutabaga, peeled and cut into 1-inch chunks

½ onion, thinly sliced

¼ cup vegetable stock

1 tbsp. extra virgin olive
oilBlack pepper

½ pound fresh cabbage, roughly chopped

Put all of the ingredients in a slow cooker except the last one. Top with handfuls of cabbage and stuff the slow cooker with it.

If you can't fit it all in at once, let the first batch cook first and add some more cabbage.

Cook for 3 or 4 hours on medium until carrots become soft. Scrape the sides and serve.

Endive & Kohlrabi in Pesto Sauce

Ingredients

1 ½ pounds kohlrabi, peeled and cut into 1-inch chunks

½ onion, thinly sliced

¼ cup vegetable stock

1 tbsp. extra virgin olive
oil2 tbsp. pesto sauce

Black pepper

½ pound fresh endive, roughly chopped

Put all of the ingredients in a slow cooker except the last one. Top with handfuls of endive and stuff the slow cooker with it.

If you can't fit it all in at once, let the first batch cook first and add some more endive.

Cook for 3or 4 hours on medium until kohlrabi become soft. Scrape the sides and serve.

Slow Cooked Turnip Greens & Yam

Ingredients

1 ½ pounds yam, peeled and cut into 1-inch chunks

½ onion, thinly sliced

¼ cup vegetable stock

1 tbsp. extra virgin olive
oil2 tbsp. pesto sauce

Black pepper

½ pound fresh turnip greens, roughly chopped

Put all of the ingredients in a slow cooker except the last one.

Top with handfuls of turnip greens and stuff the slow cooker with it. If you can't fit it all in at once, let the first batch cook first and add some more turnip greens.

Cook for 3or 4 hours on medium until yam become soft. Scrape the sides and serve.

Slow Cooked Choy Sum in Yellow Bean Sauce

Ingredients

1 ½ pounds turnips, peeled and cut into 1-inch chunks

½ onion, thinly sliced

¼ cup vegetable stock
1 tbsp. sesame seed
oil

2 tbsp. chopped green onion,
minced4 tbsp. garlic, finely minced

2 tbsp. Chinese yellow bean
sauceBlack pepper

½ pound fresh choy sum, roughly chopped

Put all of the ingredients in a slow cooker except the last one. Top with handfuls of choy sum and stuff the slow cooker with it. If you can't fit it all in at once, let the first batch cook first and addsome more choy sum.

Cook for 3or 4 hours on medium until turnips become soft. Scrape the sides and serve.

Slow Cooked Mustard Greens & Potatoes in Pesto Sauce

Ingredients

1 ½ pounds potatoes, peeled and cut into 1-inch chunks

½ onion, thinly sliced

¼ cup vegetable stock

1 tbsp. extra virgin olive
oil2 tbsp. pesto sauce

Black pepper

½ pound fresh mustard greens, roughly chopped

Put all of the ingredients in a slow cooker except the last one.

Top with handfuls of mustard greens and stuff the slow cooker with it. If you can't fit it all in at once, let the first batch cook first and add some more mustard greens.

Cook for 3 or 4 hours on medium until potatoes become soft. Scrape the sides and serve.

Slow Cooked Watercress and Chanterelle Mushrooms

Ingredients

1 ½ pounds chanterelle mushrooms

½ onion, thinly sliced

¼ cup vegetable stock

1 tbsp. extra virgin olive
oil Rainbow peppercorns

½ pound fresh watercress, roughly chopped

Put all of the ingredients in a slow cooker except the last one.
Top with handfuls of watercress and stuff the slow cooker with
it. If you can't fit it all in at once, let the first batch cook first
and add some more watercress

Cook for 3 or 4 hours on medium until mushrooms become soft.
Scrape the sides and serve.

Buttery Oyster Mushrooms and Kale

Ingredients

1 ½ pounds oyster mushrooms

½ onion, thinly sliced

¼ cup vegetable stock

2 tbsp. vegan butter or margarine 1 tsp. herbs de Provence

Black pepper

½ pound fresh kale, roughly chopped

Put all of the ingredients in a slow cooker except the last one. Top with handfuls of kale and stuff the slow cooker with it.

If you can't fit it all in at once, let the first batch cook first and add some more kale.

Cook for 3 or 4 hours on medium until mushrooms become soft. Scrape the sides and serve.

Slow-cooked Porcini Mushrooms and Watercress

Ingredients

1 ½ pounds porcini mushrooms

½ onion, thinly sliced

¼ cup vegetable
stock 1 tbsp. canola
oil

2 tbsp. minced
garlicBlack pepper

½ pound fresh watercress, roughly chopped

Put all of the ingredients in a slow cooker except the last one. Top with handfuls of watercress and stuff the slow cooker with it. If you can't fit it all in at once, let the first batch cook first and add some more watercress.

Cook for 3 or 4 hours on medium until mushrooms become soft. Scrape the sides and serve.

Slow cooked Italian-style Swiss Chard

Ingredients

1 ½ pounds crimini mushrooms

½ onion, thinly sliced

¼ cup vegetable stock

1 tbsp. extra virgin olive
oil2 tbsp. garlic

1   tsp.   Italian
seasoning   Black
pepper

½ pound fresh swiss chard, roughly chopped

Put all of the ingredients in a slow cooker except the last one. Top with handfuls of swiss chard and stuff the slow cooker with it. If you can't fit it all in at once, let the first batch cook first and add some more swiss chard.

Cook for 3 or 4 hours on medium until mushrooms become soft. Scrape the sides and serve.

Slow Cooked Shitake Mushroom and Spinach in Hoi sin Sauce

Ingredients

1 pound shitake mushrooms, coarsely chopped

½ onion, thinly sliced

¼ cup vegetable stock1 tbsp. sesame oil

2 tbsp. hoi sin sauceBlack pepper

½ pound fresh spinach, roughly chopped

Put all of the ingredients in a slow cooker except the last one.Top with handfuls of spinach and stuff the slow cooker with it.

If you can't fit it all in at once, let the first batch cook first and addsome more spinach.

Cook for 3or 4 hours on medium until mushrooms become soft. Scrape the sides and serve.

Slow Cooked Oyster Mushrooms and Spinach in Yellow BeanSauce

Ingredients

1 ½ pounds oyster mushrooms

½ onion, thinly sliced

¼ cup vegetable
stock1 tbsp. sesame
oil

2 tbsp. yellow bean
sauceBlack pepper

½ pound fresh spinach, roughly chopped

Put all of the ingredients in a slow cooker except the last one.Top with handfuls of spinach and stuff the slow cooker with it.

If you can't fit it all in at once, let the first batch cook first and addsome more spinach.

Cook for 3or 4 hours on medium until mushrooms become soft. Scrape the sides and serve.

Slow Cooked Curried Choy Sum & Button Mushrooms

Ingredients

1 ½ pounds button mushrooms

½ onion, thinly sliced

¼ cup vegetable stock

1 tbsp. extra virgin olive
oil 1 tbsp. curry powder

Black pepper

½ pound fresh choy sum, roughly chopped

Put all of the ingredients in a slow cooker except the last one. Top with handfuls of choy sum and stuff the slow cooker with it. If you can't fit it all in at once, let the first batch cook first and add some more choy sum.

Cook for 3 or 4 hours on medium until mushrooms become soft. Scrape the sides and serve.

Slow Cooked Sichuan Style Watercress & Enoki Mushrooms

Ingredients

1 ½ pounds enoki mushrooms

½ onion, thinly sliced

¼ cup vegetable stock 1 tbsp. sesame oil

1 tsp. Sichuan peppercorn Black pepper

½ pound fresh watercress, roughly chopped

Put all of the ingredients in a slow cooker except the last one. Top with handfuls of watercress and stuff the slow cooker with it. If you can't fit it all in at once, let the first batch cook first and add some more watercress.

Cook for 3 or 4 hours on medium until mushrooms become soft. Scrape the sides and serve.

Slow cooked Collard Greens & Portobello Mushrooms

Ingredients

1 ½ pounds Portobello mushrooms

½ onion, thinly sliced

¼ cup vegetable stock

1 tbsp. extra virgin olive
oil2 tbsp. pesto sauce

Black pepper

½ pound fresh collard greens, roughly chopped

Put all of the ingredients in a slow cooker except the last one.

Top with handfuls of collard greens and stuff the slow cooker with it. If you can't fit it all in at once, let the first batch cook first and add some more collard greens.

Cook for 3or 4 hours on medium until mushrooms become soft. Scrape the sides and serve.

Slow Cooked Style Turnip Greens and Chanterelle Mushrooms

Ingredients

1 ½ pounds chanterelle mushrooms

½ onion, thinly sliced

¼ cup vegetable
stock 2 tbsp. sesame
oil

2 tbsp. Thai chili garlic
paste 2 leaves Thai Basil

Black pepper

½ pound fresh turnip greens, roughly chopped

Put all of the ingredients in a slow cooker except the last one.

Top with handfuls of turnip greens and stuff the slow cooker with it. If you can't fit it all in at once, let the first batch cook first and add some more turnip greens.

Cook for 3 or 4 hours on medium until mushrooms become soft. Scrape the sides and serve.

Slow cooked Endives and Porcini Mushrooms

Ingredients

1 ½ pounds porcini mushrooms

½ onion, thinly sliced

¼ cup vegetable stock

1 tbsp. extra virgin olive
oil2 tbsp. pesto sauce

1   tsp.   Italian
seasoning   Black

pepper

½ pound fresh endives, roughly chopped

Put all of the ingredients in a slow cooker except the last one. Top with handfuls of endives and stuff the slow cooker with it.

If you can't fit it all in at once, let the first batch cook first and add some more endives.

Cook for 3 or 4 hours on medium until mushrooms become soft. Scrape the sides and serve.

Slow Mustard Greens and Enoki Mushrooms

Ingredients

1 ½ pounds enoki mushrooms

½ onion, thinly sliced

¼ cup vegetable stock

1 tbsp. extra virgin olive
oil2 tbsp. olives

2 tbsp.

capers Black

pepper

½ pound fresh mustard greens, roughly chopped

Put all of the ingredients in a slow cooker except the last one.

Top with handfuls of mustard greens and stuff the slow cooker with it. If you can't fit it all in at once, let the first batch cook first and add some more mustard greens.

Cook for 3or 4 hours on medium until mushrooms become soft. Scrape the sides and serve.

Slow Cooked Kale and Button Mushrooms

Ingredients

1 ½ pounds button mushrooms

½ onion, thinly sliced

¼ cup vegetable stock

1 tbsp. extra virgin olive
oil1 tsp. cumin

1   tsp.   annatto
seeds1 tsp. olives

Black pepper

½ pound fresh Kale, roughly chopped

Put all of the ingredients in a slow cooker except the last one. Top with handfuls of Kale and stuff the slow cooker with it.

If you can't fit it all in at once, let the first batch cook first and addsome more Kale.

Cook for 3or 4 hours on medium until mushrooms become soft.

Scrape the sides and serve.

Slow cooked Choy Sum and Shitake Mushrooms

Ingredients

1 ½ pounds shitake mushrooms

½ onion, thinly sliced

¼ cup vegetable stock

2 tbsp. sesame seed

oil1 tbsp. hoi sin sauce

1 tbsp. hoi sin

sauceBlack pepper

½ pound fresh choy sum, roughly chopped

Put all of the ingredients in a slow cooker except the last one.
Top with handfuls of choy sum and stuff the slow cooker with
it. If you can't fit it all in at once, let the first batch cook first
and addsome more choy sum.

Cook for 3or 4 hours on medium until mushrooms become soft.
Scrape the sides and serve.

Slow Cooked Romaine Lettuce and Chanterelle Mushrooms

Ingredients

1 ½ pounds chanterelle mushrooms

½ onion, thinly sliced

¼ cup vegetable stock

1 tbsp. extra virgin olive
oil 1 tsp. garlic powder

1   tsp.   onion
powder   Black
pepper

½ pound fresh romaine lettuce, roughly chopped

Put all of the ingredients in a slow cooker except the last one.

Top with handfuls of romaine lettuce and stuff the slow cooker with it. If you can't fit it all in at once, let the first batch cook first and add some more romaine lettuce.

Cook for 3 or 4 hours on medium until mushrooms become soft. Scrape the sides and serve.

Slow Cooked Mustard Greens and Porcini Mushrooms

Ingredients

1 ½ pounds porcini mushrooms

½ onion, thinly sliced

¼ cup vegetable stock

1 tbsp. melted vegan butter 1 tbsp. garlic powder

1 tbsp. lime
Black
pepper

½ pound mustard greens, roughly chopped

Put all of the ingredients in a slow cooker except the last one.

Top with handfuls of mustard greens and stuff the slow cooker with it. If you can't fit it all in at once, let the first batch cook first and add some more mustard greens.

Cook for 3or 4 hours on medium until mushrooms become soft. Scrape the sides and serve.

Slow Cooked Micro Greens in Chimichurri Sauce

Ingredients

1 ½ pounds shitake mushrooms, sliced

½ onion, thinly sliced

¼ cup vegetable stock

1 tbsp. extra virgin olive
oil 2 tbsp. chimichuri
sauce Black pepper

½ pound fresh microgreens, roughly chopped

Put all of the ingredients in a slow cooker except the last one.

Top with handfuls of microgreens and stuff the slow cooker with it. If you can't fit it all in at once, let the first batch cook first and add some more microgreens.

Cook for 3or 4 hours on medium until mushrooms become soft. Scrape the sides and serve.

Slow Cooked Turnip Greens and Enoki Mushrooms in Yellow Bean Sauce

Ingredients

1 ½ pounds enoki mushrooms

½ onion, thinly sliced

¼ cup vegetable
stock 1 tbsp. sesame

oil

2 tbsp.   yellow   bean
sauce Black pepper

½ pound fresh turnip greens, roughly chopped

Put all of the ingredients in a slow cooker except the last one.

Top with handfuls of turnip greens and stuff the slow cooker with it. If you can't fit it all in at once, let the first batch cook first and add some more turnip greens.

Cook for 3 or 4 hours on medium until mushrooms become soft. Scrape the sides and serve.

Endives and Oyster Mushroom in Chimichurri Sauce

Ingredients

1 ½ pounds oyster mushrooms

½ onion, thinly sliced

¼ cup vegetable stock

2 tbsp. extra virgin olive
oil 4 tbsp. chimichurri
sauce Black pepper

½ pound endives, roughly chopped

Put all of the ingredients in a slow cooker except the last one. Top with handfuls of endives and stuff the slow cooker with it.

If you can't fit it all in at once, let the first batch cook first and add some more endives.

Cook for 3 or 4 hours on medium until mushrooms become soft. Scrape the sides and serve.

Lentils and Sweet Potato Curry

Ingredients

3 large sweet potatoes, diced (about 6 cups)3 cups vegetable stock

1 red onion, minced

6 cloves garlic, minced

2 teaspoon each ground coriander, garam masala, and chili powder1/2 teaspoon sea salt

1 1/2 cups uncooked red lentils (masoor dal)1 can coconut milk

1 cup water

combine the sweet potatoes, vegetable stock, onion, garlic, andspices in a slow cooker.

Cook on high heat in a slow cooker for 3 hours or until vegetablesbecome soft.

Add the lentils and combine.

Cook on high for another hour and a half.Add the coconut milk.

Add water as needed.

Triple Berry Jam

Ingredients

12 oz. blueberries, pureed 12 oz. strawberries, pureed 12 oz. raspberries, pureed 1 cup honey

2 teaspoons cinnamon

1/4 teaspoon ground gingerZest of 1 lemon

Cook the blueberries on low for an hour.

Stir after an hour and cook for another 4 hours.Add the spices, honey and zest.

Remove the lid and cook for another hour.

Place all of the ingredients in a blender and puree until smooth andstore in a mason jar or container.

Refrigerate.

Slow Cooked Jambalaya

Ingredients

6 oz soy chorizo* (optional) 5 jalapeno peppers, diced

¾ cup okra, ½" inch rounds

½ red onion, diced

3 celery ribs (about 1½ cups) 4 cloves garlic, minced

1 16-oz can of Rotel (diced tomatoes & green chilies)1½ cups vegetable stock

½ tsp paprika

¼ tsp sea salt

¼ tsp ground black pepper

½ tsp cayenne pepper

3 cups cooked cilantro rice

Cook the soy chorizo on medium-high

heat. Simmer and put in the Crockpot.

Add the jalapeno pepper, red onion, celery, & garlic to the slow cooker.

Add the diced tomatoes and vegetable stock.

Add the seasoning and give the vegetables a nice stir.

Cook on low for 5 hours or on high for about 2 hours and 15 minutes.

Add the cooked rice and stir with the rest of the ingredients in the slow cooker 30 minutes before serving.

Spicy Slow Cooked Vegetarian Tacos

Ingredients

30 ounces red beans 2 cans of 15 ounces each, drained of water1 cup corn canned, frozen or fresh

3 ounces chipotle pepper in adobo sauce, chopped6 ounces tomato paste 1 can

3/4 cup Chili Sauce

2 tsp. Unsweetened Cocoa Powder1 teaspoon Ground Cumin

1/4 teaspoon Ground Cinnamon

Ingredients for Garnishing and Serving

8 taco shells hard white corn or your favorite, hard or softfavorite toppings such as lettuce, avocado, lime

Sea salt

Place all of the main ingredients in a slow cooker

Cook on low heat 3 1/2 hours or on high heat for 2 hours.

Spread the ingredients on the taco shells, hard or soft.

Top with lettuce.

Add the tomatoes, avocado, and lime. Serve with beans and rice.

Baked Baby Potatoes and Green Beans

Ingredients

2 cups baby potatoes

3 tablespoons extra virgin olive oil, divided 2 cups grape tomatoes

2 cups 1-inch cut fresh green

beans6 cloves garlic, minced

2 teaspoons dried
basil 1 teaspoon sea
salt

1 (15 ounce) can chick peas, drained and rinsed

2 teaspoons extra virgin olive oil, or to taste
(optional)Sea salt

Ground black pepper to taste

Preheat your oven to 425 degrees F.
Cover the baking pan with aluminum
foil.

Coat the potatoes with 1 tablespoon olive oil in a bowl.

Pour into the pan and roast in the oven until tender, for half an
hour.Add the tomatoes, beans, garlic, basil, and sea salt with 2
tablespoons olive oil.

Take the potatoes out of the oven and move them to one side of
thepan.

Add the tomato and green beans.

Roast until tomatoes begin to wilt for 18 minutes

more. Take it out of the oven and pour into a dish.

Add garbanzo beans, 2 teaspoons olive oil, salt and pepper.

Baked Chickpeas and Broccoli

Ingredients

cooking
spray

1 tablespoon olive oil

4 cloves garlic,
minced 1/2 teaspoon
sea salt

1/4 teaspoon ground white
pepper3 cups sliced broccoli

2 ½ cups cherry tomatoes

1 (15 ounce) can chick peas,
drained 1 small lime, cut into
wedges

1 tablespoon chopped fresh cilantro

Preheat your oven to 450 degrees F.

Line a baking pan with aluminum foil and grease with oil.

Mix the olive oil, garlic, salt, and pepper thoroughly in a bowl.

Add the broccoli, tomatoes, and garbanzo beans and combine untilwell coated.

Spread out in the baking pan.
Add the lime wedges.

Bake in the oven until vegetables are caramelized, for about 25 minutes.

Remove lime and top with cilantro.

Baked Lima Beans Summer Squash & Potatoes

Ingredients

2 (15 ounce) cans lima beans, rinsed and drained

1/2 summer squash - peeled, seeded, and cut into 1-inch pieces1 red onion, diced

2 large carrots, cut into 1 inch pieces

4 medium russet potatoes, cut into 1-inch pieces3 tablespoons olive oil

1 teaspoon sea salt

1/2 teaspoon ground black pepper1 teaspoon onion powder

1 teaspoon garlic powder

1 teaspoon ground fennel seeds1 teaspoon dried rubbed sage

2 green scallions, chopped (optional)

Preheat your oven to 350 degrees F .

Layer the beans, summer squash, onion, sweet potato, carrots, and russet potatoes on an oiled pan.

Drizzle with olive oil and coat.

Mix the salt, black pepper, onion powder, garlic powder, ground fennel seeds, and rubbed sage thoroughly in a bowl.

Sprinkle this seasoning over vegetables on a pan. Bake in the oven for 25 minutes.

Roast until vegetables are soft and lightly browned, for around 23 minutes.

Season with more salt and pepper to taste Sprinkle with chopped green onion.

Baked Carrots and Red Beets

Ingredients

2 cups mini cabbages, trimmed 1 cup large Sweet potato chunks 1 cup large carrot chunks

1 cup cauliflower florets 1 cup cubed red beets 1/2 cup shallot chunks

2 tablespoons extra virgin olive oil Sea salt

Ground black pepper to taste

Preheat your oven to 425 degrees F.

Set the rack to the second-lowest level part of the oven.

Submerge the Brussels sprouts in salted water and let it soak for 15 minutes

Drain the Brussels sprouts.

Combine the potatoes, carrots, cauliflower, beets, shallot, olive oil, salt, and pepper in a bowl.

Layer the vegetables in a single layer onto a baking sheet. Roast in the oven until caramelized for about 45 minutes.

Baked Green Beans and Sweet Potatoes

Ingredients

1 1/2 pounds sweet potatoes, cut into chunks2 tablespoons extra virgin olive oil

8 cloves garlic, thinly sliced 4 teaspoons dried rosemary 4 teaspoons dried thyme

2 teaspoons sea salt

1 bunch fresh green beans, trimmed and cut into 1 inch piecesground black pepper to taste

Preheat your oven to 425 degrees F

Combine the potatoes with 1 tbsp. of olive oil, garlic, rosemary,thyme, and 1 tsp. sea salt.

Wrap with aluminum foil.

Roast for 20 minutes in the oven.

Combine the green beans, remaining olive oil, and remaining salt.Cover, and cook for another 15 minutes, until the potatoes are tender.

Increase your oven temperature to 450 degrees F .

Take out the foil, and cook for 8 minutes, until potatoes are browned. Sprinkle with pepper.

Baked Mini Cabbage in Balsamic Glaze

Ingredients

1 (16 ounce) package fresh mini cabbage 1 small white onion, thinly sliced

5 tablespoons olive oil, divided 1/4 teaspoon sea salt

1/4 teaspoon freshly ground black pepper 1 shallot, chopped

1/4 cup balsamic vinegar

1 teaspoon chopped dried rosemary

Preheat your oven to 425 degrees F.

Mix the mini cabbage and onion thoroughly in a bowl. Add 4 tablespoons olive oil

Season with salt, and pepper
Spread the cabbage on a pan.

Bake in the oven until mini cabbage and onion become tender forabout 28 minutes.

Heat 2 tablespoons olive oil in a pan over medium-high heat. Sauté shallot until tender for about 4 minutes.

Add balsamic vinegar and cook until reduced for about 5 minutes. Add the rosemary into the glaze and pour over the vegetables.

Baked Crimini Mushrooms and Cherry Tomatoes

Ingredients

1 pound potatoes, halved

2 tablespoons extra virgin olive oil 1/2 pound cremini mushrooms

8 cloves unpeeled garlic

2 tablespoons chopped fresh thyme

1 tablespoon olive oilsea salt

ground black pepper to taste 1/4 pound cherry tomatoes

3 tablespoons toasted pine nuts1/4 pound spinach, thinly sliced

Preheat your oven to 425 degrees F .

Place the potatoes on a baking pan and drizzle with 2 tablespoonsof olive oil.

Roast for 15 minutes and turn it once.

Add the mushrooms, with the stem sides up, and garlic cloves topan.

Sprinkle with thyme and 1 tablespoon olive oilSeason with sea salt and black pepper.

Bring it back to the oven; cook 5

minutes. Add the tomatoes to the pan.

Bake until mushrooms are softened for about 5 more minutes. Sprinkle pine nuts over potatoes and mushrooms.

Garnish with sliced spinach.

Vegetarian Taco

Ingredients

1 tablespoon extra virgin olive oil1 red onion, diced

2 cloves garlic, minced

2 pcs. jalapeno, chopped

2 (14.5 ounce) cans lima beans, rinsed, drained, and mashed2 tablespoons yellow cornmeal

Seasoning Ingredients

1 1/2 tablespoons cumin

1 teaspoon Spanish paprika 1 teaspoon cayenne pepper 1 teaspoon chili powder

1 cup salsa

Heat olive oil over medium heat.

Add the onion, garlic, and jalapeno pepper and sauté until tender.Add the mashed beans.

Add the cornmeal.

Add seasoning ingredients.
Cover and cook for 5 minutes.

Vegan Winter Squash and Zucchini Fajitas

Ingredients

1/4 cup olive oil

1/4 cup red wine vinegarA Pinch of dried oregano1 teaspoon chili powder garlic salt to taste

salt and pepper to taste 1 teaspoon honey

2 small zucchini, julienned

2 medium winter squash, julienned1 large red onion, sliced

5 jalapeno peppers, minced

2 tablespoons extra virgin olive oil

1 (8.75 ounce) can whole kernel corn, drained 1 (15 ounce) can pinto beans, drained

Mix the olive oil, vinegar, oregano, chili powder, garlic salt, salt, pepper and honey thoroughly.

To this marinade add the zucchini, squash, red onion, and jalapeno peppers.

Marinate in the refrigerator for an hour or overnight. Heat the olive oil over medium-high heat.

Drain the vegetables and sauté until tender for about 12 minutes. Add the corn and beans.

Increase the heat to high until you brown the vegetables.

Spicy Curried Lima Beans

Ingredients

4 potatoes, peeled and cubed2 tablespoons olive oil

1 yellow onion, diced

6 cloves garlic, minced

1 (14.5 ounce) can diced tomatoes

1 (15 ounce) can lima beans , rinsed and drained1 (15 ounce) can peas, drained

1 (14 ounce) can coconut milkSeasoning Ingredients

2 teaspoons ground cumin

1 1/2 teaspoons cayenne pepper

1 tbsp. and 1 teaspoon curry powder 1 tbsp. and 1 teaspoon garam masala

1 (1 inch) piece fresh ginger root, peeled and minced2 teaspoons sea salt

Submerge the potatoes in salted water.

Boil over high heat and reduce heat to medium-low. Cover and let it simmer until tender, for about 15 minutes. Drain let it dry for a minute and a half.

Heat the olive oil in a skillet over medium heat.

Add the onion and garlic; cook and stir until the onion turnstranslucent for about 5 minutes.

Add the seasoning ingredients. Cook for 2 minutes more.

Stir in the tomatoes, beans, peas, and potatoes. Add the coconut milk, and simmer for 8 minutes.

Easy Steamed Asparagus

Ingredients

1 bunch asparagus spears

1 teaspoon extra virgin olive
oil 1/4 teaspoon sea salt

3 cups water

Place water in the bottom half of a steamer pan set. Add salt and oil, and bring to a boil.

Trim the dry ends off of the asparagus. If the spears are thick, peel them lightly with a vegetable peeler. Place them in the top half of the steamer pan set. Steam for 5 to 10 minutes depending on the thickness of the asparagus, or until asparagus is tender.

Steamed Broccoli

Ingredients

20 pcs. broccoli florets, preferably blanched1 teaspoon sesame seed oil

1/4 teaspoon sea salt3 cups water

Place water in the bottom half of a steamer pan set. Add salt and oil,and bring to a boil.

Place the vegetable in the top half of the steamer pan set. Steam for5 to 10 minutes depending on the thickness of the vegetable, or untilvegetable becomes tender.

Chinese Style Steamed Choy Sum

Ingredients

1 bunch choy sum

1 teaspoon sesame seed oil

1/4 teaspoon sea salt

3 cups water

Place water in the bottom half of a steamer pan set. Add salt and oil, and bring to a boil.

Place the vegetable in the top half of the steamer pan set. Steam for 5 to 10 minutes depending on the thickness of the vegetable, or until vegetable becomes tender.

Steamed Cauliflower

Ingredients

20 pcs. cauliflower florets, rinsed and drained 1 teaspoon canola oil

1/4 teaspoon sea salt 3 cups water

Place water in the bottom half of a steamer pan set. Add salt and oil, and bring to a boil.

Place the vegetable in the top half of the steamer pan set. Steam for 5 to 10 minutes depending on the thickness of the vegetable, or until vegetable becomes tender.

Easy Steamed Spinach

Ingredients

1 bunch Spinach

1 teaspoon extra virgin olive
oil 1/4 teaspoon sea salt

3 cups water

Place water in the bottom half of a steamer pan set. Add salt and oil, and bring to a boil.

Place the vegetable in the top half of the steamer pan set. Steam for 5 to 10 minutes depending on the thickness of the vegetable, or until vegetable becomes tender.

Simple Steamed Watercress

Ingredients

1 bunch watercress

1 teaspoon extra virgin olive oil1/4 teaspoon sea salt

3 cups water

Place water in the bottom half of a steamer pan set. Add salt and oil,and bring to a boil.

Place the vegetable in the top half of the steamer pan set. Steam for5 to 10 minutes depending on the thickness of the vegetable, or untilvegetable becomes tender.

Steamed Choy Sum

Ingredients

1 bunch choy sum

1 teaspoon   sesame
oil 1/4   teaspoon sea
salt 3 cups water

Place water in the bottom half of a steamer pan set. Add salt and oil, and bring to a boil.

Place the vegetable in the top half of the steamer pan set. Steam for 5 to 10 minutes depending on the thickness of the vegetable, or until vegetable becomes tender.

Vegetarian Pad ThaiSauce Ingredients 1/2 cup honey

Ingredients

1/2 cup distilled white vinegar1/4 cup soy sauce

2 tablespoons tamarind pulp

Main Ingredients

1 (12 ounce) package dried rice noodles1/2 cup sesame seed oil

2 teaspoons minced garlic4 eggs

1 (12 ounce) package firm tofu, cut into 1/2 inch strips1 tablespoon and 1 tsp. honey

1 1/2 teaspoons sea salt

1 1/2 cups ground peanuts

1 1/2 teaspoons ground, dried oriental radish1/2 cup chopped fresh chives

1 tablespoon Thai chili garlic

paste2 cups fresh bean sprouts

1 lime, cut into wedges

Over medium heat combine all of the sauce ingredientsSoak the rice noodles in cold water until soft and drain.

In a large pan, warm the olive oil, garlic and eggs over medium heat.Stir to scramble the eggs.

Add the tofu and stir

Add the noodles and stir until cooked.

Add the sauce, 1 1/2 tablespoons honey and 1 1/2 teaspoons seasalt.

Add the peanuts and ground radish.

Take it off the heat and add chives and chili garlic paste.Garnish with lime and bean sprouts.

Stir Fried Sweet Potatoes

Ingredients

1 onion, chopped

1/4 cup extra virgin olive oil

1 pound sweet potatoes, peeled and cubed1 teaspoon sea salt

Spice Mix

1/2 teaspoon cayenne

pepper 1/4 teaspoon ground turmeric 1/4 teaspoon ground cumin

2 tomatoes, chopped

Sauté and brown the onion in oil in a pan.

Add the sea salt, cayenne, turmeric and cumin.

Stir in the potatoes and cook while stirring frequently for 10 min. Stir in the tomatoes and cover

Cook until potatoes become soft, for about 11 minutes.

Vegetarian Garbanzo Bean Sandwich Filling

Ingredients

1 (19 ounce) can garbanzo beans, drained and rinsed1 stalk celery, chopped

1/2 red onion, chopped

1 tablespoon
mayonnaise1 tablespoon
lemon juice 1 teaspoon
dried dill weedSea salt

Pepper to taste

Rinse and drain the beans.

Pour the beans into a bowl and mash with a fork.

Stir in celery, onion, vegan mayonnaise , lemon juice, dill, sea saltand pepper to taste.

Simple Red Bean and Jalapeno Burrito

Ingredients

2 (10 inch) flour tortillas 2 tablespoons olive oil

1 small red onion, chopped

1/2 green bell pepper, chopped 2 teaspoon minced garlic

1 (15 ounce) can red beans, rinsed and drained 1 teaspoon minced jalapeno peppers

3 ounces ricotta cheese 1/2 teaspoon sea salt

2 tablespoons chopped fresh cilantro

Wrap tortillas in a foil

Bake them in a preheated 350 degree oven for 15 minutes. Heat oil in a pan over medium heat.

Place red onion, bell pepper, garlic and jalapenos in a pan. Cook for 2 minutes while stirring occasionally.

Pour the beans into the pan and cook for 3 minutes while constantly stirring.

Cut dairy free cream cheese into cubes and add to the pan with salt. Cook for 2 minutes while stirring.

Add cilantro into this mixture.

Spoon this evenly on the center of every warmed tortilla and roll the tortillas up.

Vegetarian Sloppy Joe

Ingredients

1 tablespoon oil, or as needed 1/2 red onion, minced

1/2 red bell pepper, minced

¼ cup minced garlic1 cup water

3/4 cup ketchup

3 tablespoons spicy brown mustard

2 tablespoons soy sauce

2 tablespoons vegan barbeque sauce (ex. Simple Girl Organic)1 tablespoon maple syrup

1 tablespoon Tabasco or Frank's hot sauce1 teaspoon thyme

1 teaspoon cayenne pepper, or to taste

2 cups cooked garbanzo beans, or more to taste

Heat oil in a pan over medium heat.

Sauté the onion, red bell pepper, and garlic until tender for about 10 minutes.

Add the water, ketchup, mustard, soy sauce, barbeque sauce, honey, hot sauce, thyme, and cayenne pepper to the mixture. Boil this mixture.

Reduce heat and simmer until sauce thickens, for about 5 minutes. Add the beans into the sauce and simmer until beans are warmed.

Ramen and Tofu Stir Fry with Sweet and Sour Sauce

Ingredients

1 (3.5 ounce) package ramen noodles (such as Nissin(R) TopRamen)

3 tablespoons sesame seed oil1 slice firm tofu, cubed

1/2 thai bird chillies, chopped

1/4 small red onion, chopped 1/3 cup plum sauce

1/3 cup sweet and sour sauce

Boil a pot of lightly salted water.

Cook the noodles in boiling water and stir occasionally, until noodlesare tender but still firm to the bite, 2 to 3 minutes.

Drain the noodles.

Heat oil in a pan over high heat.

Place the tofu on one side of the pan.

Place the chilies and the red onion on the other side of the pan. Cook a tofu until browned on all sides for 2 minutes.

Cook and stir onion and pepper until browned, 2 minutes. Stir in the noodles into the pan

Combine the noodles, tofu, onion, and pepper.

Pour the plum sauce and sweet and sour sauce over the noodle. Sauté until well-combined for 3 minutes.

Vegetarian Quinoa and Chickpea Burger

Ingredients

1 1/2 cups cooked quinoa

2 tablespoons Dijon mustard

1 egg vegan (Brand: Follow Your Heart Egg Vegan), beaten2 cloves garlic, minced

2 grinds fresh black pepper

1/2 cup chickpea (garbanzo bean) flour, or as needed2 teaspoons olive oil, or as needed

2 slices gouda cheese

Combine the quinoa, mustard, vegan egg, garlic, and black peppertogether in a bowl; add enough chickpea flour to make 2 patties.

Heat oil in a pan over medium heat

Cook patties in oil until browned for around 4 minutes per side.Add a vegan cheese slice to each patty and warm until cheesemelts, about 2 and a half minutes.

Spicy Curried Purple Cabbage

Ingredients

3 tablespoons olive oil

2 dried red chili peppers, broken into pieces 2 tsp. skinned split black lentils (urad dal)

1 teaspoon split Bengal gram (chana dal)1 teaspoon mustard seed

1 sprig fresh curry leaves

1 pinch asafoetida powder

4 green chili peppers, minced

1 head purple cabbage, finely chopped 1/4 cup frozen peas (optional)

salt to taste

1/4 cup grated coconut

Heat the oil in pan on medium-high heat

Fry the red peppers, lentils, Bengal gram, and mustard seed in theoil.

When the lentils begin to brown, add the curry leaves and asafoetidapowder and stir.

Add the green chili peppers and cooking for a minute more.Combine the cabbage and peas into this mixture.

Season with sea salt.

Cook until the cabbage wilts, for about 10 minutes.

Add the coconut to the mixture and cook for 2 minutes more.

Conclusion

How did you like these delicious vegetarian recipes? If your passion for cooking is strong then I'm sure you will like them.

Unfortunately this book is finished but there will soon be many others, always full of new and delicious vegetarian recipes.

always remember that the best combination to accentuate the benefits of a vegetarian diet is to avoid having a sedentary lifestyle and to do a lot of sport. We send you a big greeting. See you soon.

Lightning Source UK Ltd.
Milton Keynes UK
UKHW050003060421
381487UK00006B/255